Dr. Isaac K. Damoah

Respect the heroes

Dr. Isaac K. Damoah

Respect the heroes

The faith of the early disciples

Blessed Hope Publishing

Imprint
Any brand names and product names mentioned in this book are subject to trademark, brand or patent protection and are trademarks or registered trademarks of their respective holders. The use of brand names, product names, common names, trade names, product descriptions etc. even without a particular marking in this work is in no way to be construed to mean that such names may be regarded as unrestricted in respect of trademark and brand protection legislation and could thus be used by anyone.

Cover image: www.ingimage.com

Publisher:
Blessed Hope Publishing
is a trademark of
Dodo Books Indian Ocean Ltd. and OmniScriptum S.R.L publishing group

120 High Road, East Finchley, London, N2 9ED, United Kingdom
Str. Armeneasca 28/1, office 1, Chisinau MD-2012, Republic of Moldova, Europe
Printed at: see last page
ISBN: 978-620-4-18821-8

RESPECT THE HEROES

BY:

DR. ISAAC K. DAMOAH

DEDICATION

I dedicate this book to the blessed memory of my late father, Mr. Joseph K. Damoah.

ACKNOWLEDGEMENT

From the bottom of my heart, I sincerely express my gratitude to the Almighty God for giving me knowledge and wisdom to write this book. May His name be glorified. I thank the authors of the various books that consulted. Had it not been their help this book wouldn't have become wholesome. I thank the individuals who encouraged me to write this book. I once again give thanks to everyone who will read this book.

PREFACE

The title of the book is "Respect the heroes", introduction is brief introduction to church history and talks about original disciples of Jesus Christ, how the early church began, when the early church started, history of the early church, importance of the study of church history, church fathers, the first church building, apostolic fathers, names of apostolic fathers, the life of the twelve apostles of Christ, professions of the original apostles of Christ, a disciple, spiritual leaders who had disciples, reasons why spiritual leaders need disciples, spiritual father, responsibilities of spiritual father, benefits from spiritual father, church, reasons why we go to church, godparent, the role of godparent, a martyr, reasons why the early Christians were martyred, the famous martyrs, the Peterine cross, prayer, importance of prayer, homosexuality, masturbation, the death of apostle Paul, incest, abortion, prostitution, lottery and Bible verses about holiness, prayer, repentance, salvation, forgiveness, , faith, the Lord's Supper, patience, church, water baptism, sin, Holy Spirit, Trinity, sons of God, children of the Devil, evangelism, vigilance, , existence of God, Jesus Christ, Satan, guardian angels and Heaven.

TABLE OF CONTENTS

INTRODUCTION

Church history is an academic course which deals with the history of Christianity and how Christian church advanced since it's inception. According to Henry Melviil Gwatkin church history is the spiritual aspect of the history of civilized people until Jesus' coming. A. M Renwick says church history is a record of the church's victory and failure in fulfilling Christ Great Commission project. Renwick proposes fourfold divisions of church history namely, missionary activity, church organization, doctrines and the effect on man's life. Church history is not always study from Christian perspective. Authors from different church traditions often accept people and events specifically important to their own denominational history. Catholic and Orthodox authors admit the accomplishment of ecumenical council, evangelical historians concentrate on the Protestant Reformation and the Great Awakenings.

CHAPTER ONE

THE ORIGINAL APOSTLES OF JESUS CHRIST

The names of the original apostles of Jesus Christ are Peter, James, John, Andrew, Philip, Judas Iscariot, Matthew, Thomas, James, the son of Alpheus, Bartholomew, Judas Thaddeus and Simon Zelotes. Jesus Christ called Peter as "Rock" and through him He established His church. The apostles of Jesus Christ were twelve people who came from different backgrounds. He called them to assist Him to preach the gospel and to serve humanity. The apostles were chosen by God to perform His priesthood and were ordained to hold His authority. They were the foundation stones of His church and many of them wrote the books of the New Testament Bible. In Revelation 21: 14 says the twelve foundations of the wall of the new Jerusalem will consist of the names of the twelve apostles. The 12 apostles were main leaders in Christian religion. and assisted to proclaim the gospel throughout the world. Four Biblical texts mention the names of the apostles (Matthew 10: 2-4; Mark 3: 16-19; Luke 6: 12-16; Acts 1: 13). The list of the names of the apostles in the synoptic gospel is referring to the time Jesus called them into His ministry. He officially appointed them as His apostles. The names of the apostles found in Acts refers to when Jesus ascended to Heaven and the believers planned to replace Judas Iscariot while waiting for the promise of the Holy Spirit.

WHO IS AN APOSTLE

The word "apostle" comes from the Greek word "apostolos" meaning "one who is sent" or "one commissioned". The word "apostle is repeated over 80 times in the New Testament Bible. The term "apostle" mentioned in Hebrews is referring to Jesus Christ who was sent by God. The New Testament Bible specifies two usage of the term "apostle". The first is referring to the twelve apostles of Christ but the second usage refers to individual Christians who are sent out as messengers of the gospel. In the New Testament times the twelve apostles hold special position. They were the first messengers of the gospel after Jesus rose from the dead. They were the foundation of the early church and Jesus Christ was the cornerstone (Ephesi1stans 2: 20). In the first century the qualification to become an apostle are: 1. The person must witness about Jesus' resurrection (1Corinthians 9: 1). 2. He or she should be selected by the Holy Spirit (Acts 9: 15). 3. The fellow must be capable to perform signs and wonders (Acts 2: 43; 2Corinthians 12: 12). Besides, Jesus' apostles in the generic sense, there are apostles especially Barnabas is an apostle (Acts 13: 2; 14: 14). During Jesus' earthly ministry in the 1st century AD, they were His closet disciples and were the instructors of the gospel. According to the gospel of Luke Eastern Christian tradition confirms that there are 70 apostles during Jesus' earthly ministry. After His resurrection, He sent 11 apostles to preach His doctrines to all nations. This event is known as "dispersion of the apostles". Paul address himself as an apostle of Jesus in his letters. Later he addressed himself as an apostle to the genitals.

HOW DID THE EARLY CHURCH BEGIN

The early church started in Jerusalem and developed out of the Jewish tradition. Jesus Christ and His disciples were Jews. The early followers of Christ did not meet in separate churches but gathered in the local Jewish Synagogues. Apostle Paul was among the main leaders of the early church and accepted that the gospel of Christ was for mankind but not written for the Jews only. This belief compelled him to establish churches in the entire Roman Empire including Europe and Africa.

WHEN DID THE EARLY CHURCH START

The early church started on the Pentecost Day. That is fifty days after the Passover when Jesus passed away and resurrected from the dead. The word "church" in Greek means "called out from the world for God". The word "church " in the Bible refers to those who are born again (John 3: 3) base on the faith of Jesus' death and resurrection (Romans 10: 9-10). The word "church " is first found in Matthew 16: 18. The book of the Acts of the apostles gives an account of the beginning of the early church and how it spread the gospel through the power of the Holy Spirit. Ten days after Jesus' ascension to Heaven (Acts 1: 9), the Holy Spirit baptized 120 followers of Jesus (Acts 1: 15; 2: 1-4). The disciples who were afraid to show that Jesus was their master were empowered by the Holy Spirit to preach the gospel of Christ.

THE HISTORY OF THE EARLY CHURCH

1 - 500 AD

From the earliest centuries of the church shows that the disciples of Jesus Christ followed His doctrines wholeheartedly. They did not allow political persecution, disparity between diverse cultures or tension of doctrinal disputes to hinder them from spreading Christianity. Around 52AD apostle Thomas had preached the gospel of Christ in Western India. He died as a martyr 20years later. His death brought the celebration of his grave worshipped by tombstone in the middle of 4th century especially Indians honoring the Hebrew Saints. This cross-cultural likeness is a emblem of Christian descriptions beginning from the clean-shaven, Apollo-esque Good Shepherd culminating a Roman Catacomb fresco through 15th century Ethiopian illumination of Saint Mark with pen and bookmaking. The early church focused on missions, yielded, under covered and retained historical link with Jesus Christ. By the end of 1st century non of the apostles of Christ existed and many of them died as a martyr. All the apostles had died ; Christians portrayed their deaths for the next two millennia.

Medival manuscript (879-883, Byzantine) That is characteristics compilation of apostolic martyrdoms. In 12th century a Russian church fresco regarded Paul as an apostle because he met Christ on his way to Damasco. Apostle Paul was beheaded by the Roman Emperor but apostle Peter perceived that he did not deserve to die like the way Jesus gave up the ghost. Around AD 70 Roman general in the person of Titus demoralized the first Jewish Revolt. After snatching Jerusalen from revolutionary government, he ransacked and burned the temple portraying rebellion which ended the Jewish temple worship. After eleven years, Domitian built an Arch of Titus to recall Romans' victory over regional coup. The interior walls are still existing symbolizing Titus moving victoriously home and defilement of the temple. The 1st century Jews were astonished that the liturgical instrument utilized for worship about hundreds of years like the golden lampstand (Exodus 25). This instrument used in the tabernacle served as monument by Roman soldiers. The monument was not found in Jerusalen but in Pagan Rome. Authors like Justin Martyr perceived this defilement as a mark of divine rejection of the Jews. He stated this in his manuscript around 4th century. That idea would promote Christian antisemitism for millennia. The booting of Jerusalen compelled the early church to preach the gospel outside the hometown of Jesus Christ. According to Alexamenos Graffito Christians endure both persecution and mockery.

SIGNIFICANCE OF THE STUDY OF CHURCH HISTORY

Part of a large family of faith: Sometimes Christians think the church started at the reformation time. We forget ourselves that there has been a remnant and a true church. Christ assured us that the gate of Hell would not prevail against His church and the gate of Hell had not defeated His church. Jesus Christ dwelled in the early church and people loved Him. People like Irenaeus, Athanasius, Augustine, in the middle age Thomas Acquinas, Anselem, during the reformation era Luthur, Calvin, in the early modern times Edwards, Whitefield and in the modern times Machen, Henry, Barth. Church history helps Christians to change our old mentality such as our denomination is right and other denominations are always wrong. A lot of denominations are not 400years old. This reminds that we belong to large family of faith which is over 2000years.

Helps to interprets the Bible: The word of God must be explained within a community of faith. When a person turns from the church doctrines , the fellow has become cult. As believers in Christ, we should explain the Scripture as we get ideas and never acquire ideas from the people around us. We utilize the larger community of faith comprising of the writings of Christian brothers and sisters who are dead.

Correct doctrines: When it comes to Biblical interpretation, people of God may explain certain doctrines wrongly such as Trinity, the deity of Jesus Christ, the resurrection and the second coming of Jesus. Church history enables us to know what Christians believe and the doctrines they regard most important. It assists us to pass on Jesus' gospel to the next generation (Jude 1: 3). As the saying goes "new kinds of Christians are really just old kinds of heretics". Acquiring knowledge about correct doctrines helps us to fight against false teachers and religious sects.

Helps to guard against reading our culture into the Biblical text: Church history assists us to understand how other cultures have explained the Bible. Through this, we discover our biases and prejudices. For example, topics like homosexuality and gender roles are debatable subjects but most of the churches have accepted them as normal.

Defined tradition: It is vital to know the belief system of the church and find out why. This prevents us from "drinking the Kool-Aid" and just follow what our denomination says.

Assists to address situation: All the problems we are facing today had been encountered by the early Christians. The old age says those who refuse to study history are doomed to repeat it. It helps to learn the good deeds of the early Christians and avoid the mistakes they committed.

Understand the Bible and avoid theological mistakes: Marcion was a second century heretic who failed to unite the God of the Old Testament with gracious and loving Jesus of the New Testament. He generalized that there were two gods namely, pathetic and insufferable "bad god" who made the world and the kind and gentle "good god". That is Jesus Christ who delivered man from the "bad god"

Continue story of God working in His people: Right from the fall of Adam and Eve in the Garden of Eden through the new covenant by the blood of Jesus. Church history is the progressive story of divine grace working in His church.

THE ROLE CHRISTIAN WOMEN PLAYED IN THE 1ST CENTURY

Prominence of women: The records of the early church and the writings of the church fathers show how women were prominent in the early church. The New Testament Bible indicates vital part women played in the establishment of Christianity. After Jesus' ascension, women met the apostles and other disciples in the upper room in Jerusalen. Women played important role in the sharing of the gospel of Christ.

The writings of the early church fathers: Christianity established the sanctity of the whole family which makes marital relationship to be union of Christ with His church. A woman is no more a slave of man and the tool of lust. The writings of the early church portray the New Testament's doctrines with respect to women's role. Polycarp as a apostolic father (AD69-155) who died aa a martyr indicated the duties of wives. He advised them to abide in the faith, kept themselves pure and love their husbands in the truth and trained their children in the knowledge and fear of God. Ignatius (died c AD107) instructed husbands to love their wives as their own bodies and fellow-slaves of God; being partners of life and co-adjutors in producing children. The Shepherd of Hermas talked about infidelity and divorce. He told men that if they recall their own wives, they would not sin. Titan (AD110-172) told the Greeks to compare heathen and Christian women and wrote that all the women were chaste but the maidens at their distaffs singing glory songs. In AD153-217 Clement of Alexandria defined the role of women and gave orders concerning their duties and conducts

The Influence of Women

Wives and Mothers: Godly women contribute to the development of Christian faith in their family members. A lot of church fathers influenced the faith of godly mothers. Theodoret (AD300) had respectable and devoted mother. Basil the great (AD329) her mother feared God and her grandmother was God-fearing. Both of the parents influenced the life of her brother, Gregory of Nyssa. Through patience, Nona prayed for the conversion of her husband and son in AD330.

As Martyrs: It is undisputable fact that faith and boldness demonstrated by women as martyrs of the church assisted to build their esteem and influence. Clement of Alexandria wrote a chapter in "the stromata" that women and men were martyred. The history of the early church talks about women who sacrificed their lives for Christ. History says that Agnes, a thirteen-year-old girl confessed and she was killed by the sword. Caecilia, the legendary virgin who witnessed under Marcus Aurelius and Blandina, a Gallic slave demonstrated divine strength during torture and was thrown into wild beast. Biblia of lyon first retracted and later confessed. Noble women such as Irene, Casia, Philippia, Eutychia and Soter died at the time of Diocletian persecuation (AD303-313). During the reign of Valerius, Quinta was stonned and Appolonia was burned (AD257-261). Ammonarion, Mercuria and Dionysia passed away in chains. During the persecution of Decius, Fortunata, Credula, Hereda and Julia died in prison of starvation (AD 250-260). Church fathers, Cyprian; Quartillosia honored Collecta, Emerita, Calpurnia, Maria and her sisters, Januaria, Datira and Donata but Tertullas and Antonia died with him in AD250. Around 304 eighteen women died.

In society and state: At that time Christian women were able to bring others to the Christian faith. In the highest classes of society even at the emperor's court Christian women were there and had great influcene. The wife of consul Augustus

Plautinus (AD58) was the first high-ranking woman to be accused of the Christian faith. The two cousins of emperor, Domitian (AD81-96), Flavius Clemens and his wife, Flavius Domitilla were accused of "atheisem", that is Christianity. The husband was sentenced to death and the wife was exiled.

WHO ARE CHURCH FATHERS?

The terms "church fathers", "early church fathers" and "Christian fathers" were ancient and influential Christian theologians and authors that established the intellectual and doctrinal foundations of Christianity. The historical period they worked is called the "patristic era" and it began in the late 1st to mid-8th centuries, progressing during 4th and 5th centuries when Christianity was officially recognized as the state church of the Roman Empire. A lot of Christian denominations considered the writings of the Ante-Nicene Fathers, Nicene Fathers and post Nicene Fathers among the holy tradition. According to traditional dogmatic theology writers esteemed church fathers as authorities for the establishment of doctrines. Church fathers like Origen and Tertullian contributed to the advancement of later Christian theology but certain aspect of their doctrines were condemned. The term "church father is utilized for the intellectual leaders of the church and not referring to the Saints. It does not only refer to the New Testament authors but also includes heretic authors.

THE FIRST CHURCH BUILDING

After the ascension of Jesus Christ, Christianity began as religion and Christians did not meet in church building but gathered in houses. This is called home churches. In the first fifty years after Jesus' ascension Christians gathered in homes because of finance. The money they got were utilized to assist poor Christians, missionaries and clergy. When Christianity developed, the Roman Empire persecuted Christians. Due to this, believers could not put up church building but secretly gathered and held meetings in peoples' home. Many of the New Testament books confirm this issue (Acts 20: 20; 1Corinthians 16: 19). The book of Philemon, II and III John also talk about home churches. Ceremonies of communion and baptism took place in the room using table for communion and basin to sprinkle water. Baptism by immersion occurred in a river because houses were lacking tubes. Around 230 in Dura-Europos in Southeastern Syira the first church building was discovered. It was a house which shared walls with surrounding houses and was turned into church building. The church had fresco on the wall. Long table at the end of the house was utilized for communion and pool was found at the center for baptism.

CHAPTER TWO

THE APOSTOLIC FATHERS

The term "apostolic father" is referring to Greek Christian authors of the early Christian works from late 1st and early 2nd centuries. Their works are the main source of information concerning Christianity during two or three generations following the apostles. They were known as "apostolic men". The word "Apostolici" was derived from through contact with the apostles or the apostolic community. The term "apostolic father" was first utilized in 6th century after the idea of the authority of the fathers had been advanced. The term "apostolic fathers" was not rampant until 17th century. The writings of the apostolic fathers are called "patristic literature". The following are the writings of the apostolic fathers: Didache, the leBarnabastter, the Shepherd of Hermas, the first letter of Clement; the second letter of Clement, the seven letters of St. Ignatius of Antioch.

NAMES OF APOSTOLIC FATHERS

– St. Clement of Rome

– St. Ignatius of Antioch

– St. Polycarp of Smyrna

– Hermas

– St. Papias of Hierapolis

– Anonymous writers of the Didache

– Quadratus of Athens

DESCRIPTION OF APOSTOLIC FATHERS

Apostolic Fathers were Christian leaders and writers who took over after the death of the apostles. Their writings were recorded between AD 80 and AD 180. Many of the apostolic fathers confirmed that they were linked with the apostles. Polycarp was a follower of apostle John. Clement was the second, third or fourth bishop of Rome and might have known some of the apostles. The apostolic fathers are also called "Ante-Nicene Fathers" and Christian theologians among the church fathers who lived in the 1st and 2nd centuries AD. Their writings widely spread in early Christianity era but were not included in the canon of the New Testament.

THE LIFE OF JESUS' ORIGINAL APOSTLES

Jesus Christ chose twelve apostles from His early disciples as His closest companions. After intensive discipleship training and when He rose from the dead, He commissioned the apostles to expand His kingdom and spread the gospel to the world (Matthew 28: 16-2; Mark 16: 15). The apostles were the pillars of the New Testament Church but their lives were full of faults and shortcomings. None of the apostles was a scholar and rabbi. They lacked extraordinary skills and were ordinary people. God appointed them for particular purpose and used them to manifest Himself.

Peter: He was a disciple who walked on the Sea through faith in Christ. Along the line He sink because he was doubting. He was impulsive, emotional but denied Jesus Christ.   Jesus loved him and he held special place among the twelve apostles. He was a spokesman for the twelve apostles, stands out in the gospel. When the names of the apostles are listed, Peter's name appears first. Peter, James and John were the inner circle apostles of Christ. They had the chance to experience the transfiguration and extraordinary revelations of Jesus. When Jesus rose from the dead, Peter became bold evangelist, missionary and one of the greatest leaders of the early church.

Andrew: Andrew left John the Baptist and followed Jesus as His first disciple but John the Baptist did not bother. John the Baptist understood that it was his duty to direct people to Jesus. Andrew stayed under the shadow of his popular brother, Simon Peter. The gospel writers state that Andrew is Peter's brother. Through Andrew, Peter became Jesus' disciple.

James: James was an early disciple of Jesus. James the son of Zebedee often called to differentiate him from the apostle named James. He was among the inner circle apostles of Christ. James and John receive nickname from the Lord Jesus as "sons of thunder. They were at the front and center of three supernatural events in the life of Christ.

John: John was a brother of James and Jesus nickname him as one of the sons of thunder but preferred to call himself the disciple whom Jesus loved. John was the younger brother of James. He had fiery temperament and was committed to Jesus. He was among the inner circle apostles of Christ.

Philip: Philip was one of the first disciples of Christ and Nathanael called him to come and see Jesus. He plays major role in the gospel of John than the rest of the gospels. He told Jesus to show them the Father and they would be content (John 14: 8-9). We don't know much about him after Jesus' ascension.

Bartholomew: Bartholomew experienced a grating first encounter with Jesus. Apostle Philip called him to come and see the Messiah. He was skeptical but followed and Philip introduced him to Jesus. Bartholomew was faithful disciple of Jesus.

Matthew: Matthew was called Levi and became an apostle of Christ. He was a custom officer in Capernaum and taxed import and exports based on his own judgement. The Jews dislike him because he worked for Roman government and betrayed his brethren. When Jesus told Matthew to follow Him, he obeyed without asking questions.

Thomas: Thomas was called "Doubting Thomas" because he did not accept that Jesus had raisen from the dead until he saw and touched Christ's wounds. He was prone to extremes. He manifested faith desiring to risk his life to follow Jesus to Judea.

James the less: James the less is an obscure apostle in the Scripture. He was present in the upper room at Jerusalem after Jesus' ascension to Heaven.

Simon the Zealot: The Bible tells us nothing about Simon the Zealot and his name is stated in three places in the gospel. He was with the apostles in the upper room after Jesus' ascension to Heaven.

Thaddeus: Thaddeus was among the least known followers. He was tender-hearted, gentle and portrayed child-like humanity.

Judas Iscariot: Judas Iscariot betrayed Jesus through kiss.

PROFESSIONS OF THE TWELVE APOSTLES OF JESUS CHRIST

Andrew, Peter, James and John: These apostles of Christ were fishermen (Matthew 4: 18-22).

Nathaniel: The Bible does not specify his occupation before he meets Jesus Christ.

Matthew: He worked as a tax collector for the Roman government.

Simon the Zealot: He involved in politics and anarchy attempted to overthrow the Roman government.

Judas Iscariot: The Bible does not specify his profession before he became an apostle of Christ.

Philip, Bartholomew and Thomas: The Scripture does not identify their professions.

DEFINITION OF A DISCIPLE

A disciple is a Christian who is following the footsteps of Christ and committed to His mission. A disciple is a committed follower. A disciple is a person who has dedicated his life to follow the doctrines of a leader. The word "stateddisciple" is once in the Old Testament Bible which is translated from the Hebrew word "limmuwd" (Isaiah 8: 16). According to the New Testament Bible the terms "disciple" and "disciples" are translated from the Greek word "mathetes". The word "mathetes" refers to a learner, pupil or an apprentice. A disciple is an individual who follows the doctrines of another person and adopt them as his rules of life and conduct.

SPIRITUAL LEADERS WHO HAD DISCIPLES

Jesus Christ: A lot of people followed Jesus Christ as the promised Messiah.

Prophet Moses: The Pharisees were the disciples of prophet Moses (John 9: 28; Matthew 23: 2-3).

Prophet Isaiah: He had followers but their names were not mentioned in the Bible (Isaiah 8: 16).

Pharisees: They had followers who involved in planning evil against Jesus Christ (Matthew 22: 15-16)

John the Baptist: The disciples of John the Baptist were genuine -hearted people (Matthew 11: 2-3; 9: 14; 11: 12; John 1: 35-37).

Prophet Elijah: Elisha was the disciple of prophet Elijah (1 Kings 19: 19-21; 2kings 2: 1-13).

Prophet Jeremiah: Baruch was the disciple of prophet Jeremiah (Jeremiah 36: 4-10; 36: 11-18).

REASONS WHY SPIRITUAL LEADERS NEED DISCIPLES

- Disciples help their master to accomplish his ministry. They continue the ministry of their master when he is not alive (Matthew 28: 19-20; Acts 1: 18; Mark 16: 15)

- They are custodian (Isaiah 8: 16)

- They serve their master (Matthew 26: 17-19; 21: 2-7; Mark 11: 2-7; Luke 19: 30-35)

WHO IS A SPIRITUAL FATHER

The term "spiritual fathers" is not found in the Bible but there are passages that talk about believers being sons to those who are over us in the Lord. Apostle Peter called Mark as his son (1Peter 5: 13). Apostle Paul called Timothy as his son in the faith (1Timothy 1: 2). In Apostle Paul's epistles he called Onesimus as his son (Philemon 1: 10). The apostles confirm that they are spiritual fathers to various congregation. Apostle John called a lot of churches he managed as his children (1John 2: 1, 12-13). Apostle Paul's relationship with the Corinthian church is just the same as a father and his children (2Corinthians 12: 14-15; 2Corinthians 4: 14-15). Spiritual father is a person God has brought in the lives of His people to assist us to establish in the Christian faith. We should learn to humble ourselves to and honor them. In Christ they serve as the source of life. The Father of Jesus Christ is God and Jesus Christ has the same nature as His Father. The body of Christ has the same relationship since we are made in His image. The word "sonship" is not only referring to God but leaders who have control over us in the Lord. Spiritual fathers are more than "godparent"(John 5: 19: 17: 20; 1Corinthians 4: 16; Titus 1: 4; Galatians 4: 7).

RESPONSIBILITIES OF SPIRITUAL FATHER

- Spiritual father should warn his children to refrain from things that will separate them from God (1Corinthians 4: 14; 4: 8-10).

- Spiritual father urges his children to follow good examples in the Bible (Hebrews 3: 13; 10: 25).

- Spiritual father live by the Bible and expects his children to his footsteps as an example (1Corinthians 4: 16-17).

- Spiritual father must discipline his children so that they would follow the Bible (1Corinthians 4: 18).

BENEFITS FROM SPIRITUAL FATHER

As children of God, we will feel secure because our spiritual fathers love us. In the atmosphere of love and acceptance there is empowerment. We can grow in the Lord and overcome our limitations. He will encourage and strengthen his children to move forward in their Christian journey. True spiritual father would treat his children as brethren in Christ which create healthy atmosphere of respect and honor. He has learned that he was God's son before fathering someone as a son on the earth. His life is a model to his children. The relationship between spiritual father and his children is not under restriction but freedom. So that his life will not be a hinderance to his children's spiritual growth. He provide sanity and sound thinking through what he shares with his children. His views about God and experiences with Him compelled his children to make changes in their lives. He assists his children to grow, mature unto perfection and release impartation on them.

CHAPTER THREE

WHAT IS CHURCH

The early disciples of Christ did not meet in a building like what we have today. The first century Christians were persecuted and met in secret places like homes. When Christianity spread, buildings that were dedicated to worship became established. In this case church comprises of people and not buildings. Fellowship, worship and ministry are organized by people. Church is the body of Christ with particular nature and purpose.

WHY DO WE GO TO CHURCH

As human, we go to church to demonstrate our love to God. It is where we meet together to show faith and trust in Him (Matthew 10: 32-33). It is a place where we can praise, thank and honor Him (Psalms 22: 22). We go to church so that we can serve Him because He deserves to be honored with service and devotion (Psalms 134: 2; Revelation 4: 11). Attending church builds us spiritually. Hearing and understanding the word of God build our spiritual life (Romans 10: 17). We experience the presence of God when we come together to worship Him. If we meet together, Christ touches the hearts of His people (Matthew 18: 20). It strengthens relationship with fellow believers in Christ. When we meet together in church, it impacts Christian fellowship. Healthy relationship with God demands fellowship with God and fellowship with other Christians. It is impossible to love God without demonstrating love to our brethren (Matthew 6: 15; John 2: 9 -10). We go to church to demonstrate love toward others in the form of fellowship. Loving our brethren in Christ helps us to humble ourselves before God. Attending church is the act of obedience to God (Hebrews 10:24-26). When we come together in the form of a church, it assists and motivates one another. If we refuse to go church, then we rejecting one of the duties Christ instructed us (James 4: 7). Through church fellowship, we perceive the need to follow the authority of spiritual leadership (Hebrews 13: 17). It helps our prayer life to develop. According to Bible when we pray together with our brethren we experience special favor with God (Matthew 18: 19). Our faith in Christ grows when we pray and worship God together (Leviticus 26: 8). It is the act of honoring the Lord's Day (Revelation 1: 10) Jesus Christ rose from the dead on the first day of week, Sunday.

Because of this, the early disciples of Christ met on Sunday to worship the Lord. Jewish Christians regard Sunday as a Sabbath Day and the resurrection day of Christ Jesus (Acts 20: 7; 1Corinthians 16: 2).

REASONS WHY PEOPLE REFUSE TO ATTEND CHURCH

Physical reasons: Many people do not want to go to church due to factors such as exhaustion, illness, disease or chronic pain. Sometimes the spirit is desiring but the flesh is weak (Matthew 26: 41).

Spiritual reasons: Others attribute the cause of not attending church to spiritual forces. The pleasures of the world have taken control of their hearts. Because of this, they have lost interest in the things of God (Psalms 42: 5).

Recreational reasons: Problems like marital problem, broken friendship and awkward personality make people lose interest in going to church. A lot of people are widow, have disagreement with a leader and created lasting tension, judged or rebuked and cause anger and shame.

Logistical reasons: Some people live at far distance or working hours change from week to week. Many mothers find it hard to bring their children to church.

Preferential reasons: Some don't like the music, liturgy, how people dress and the leadership style.

- Others see the weekend as time for hobbies, adventure, travel or kids' sports programme.

- Pastors don' close early and church service is boring.

- Pastors often preach hell and damnation.

- Pastors are more concern about money and the church is full of hypocrites.

- Pastors are not trustworthy but the church is just like cult.

- Pastors don't proclaim the gospel but have become politicians.

WHO IS GODPARENT

Godparent is a person who testifies about a child's baptism and prepared to assist his pedagogy and lasting spiritual formation. In religious and civil views godparent is an individual who is chosen by parents to train, develop, mentor or claim legal protection of the child in case anything happen to the parents. If a godparent is a male, then he is called godfather. A female godparent is known as godmother. The child is called godchild. That is godson for boys and goddaughter for girls.

THE ROLE OF GODPARENT

- Godparent make promises to godchild to help him to grow in the Christian faith and to understand how to make life as Christian.

- Speak to him concerning the bigger questions of life such as hope, faith and love.

- Model and encourage him to advance Christian values like kindness, compassion and justice.

- Pray for him to be strong in the Lord and successful in all his undertakings.

- Educate him about how to make good choices in life and for other people. That is talk to him about how to be healthy, resist temptations and control peer pressure.

- Teach him more about the Christian faith, attend church with and educate him about how to pray.

WHAT DOES IT MEAN TO DIE AS A MARRYR

According to history hundreds of the early disciples encountered persecution because of their faith in Christ. Many Christians admitted that the Roman Catholic Church was established through martyrdom of it's members. A Christian martyr is a child of God who has died for faith in Christ rather than denying the gospel. Christians who were ready to die for their faith faced punishment like crucifixion, beheading, stoning and burning.

REASON WHY THE EARLY CHRISTIANS WERE MARTYRED

Romans were polytheistic and included Greek gods and many foreign cults. The earliest form of Roman religion was animistic and people accepted that spirits inhabit everything around them. Because of this, the Romans developed hatred towards people who had different views against their religion. When the Jews and Christians were not prepared to follow Roman's belief and to offer sacrifices in their temples were regarded as a threat to the empire. As Christianity spread widely throughout the empire, persecution towards the church became common. Before the middle of the third century, the Roman Empire started public execution of the members of Catholic Church.

THE FAMOUS MARTYRS

Stephen: He was the first disciple of Christ to die as a martyr in 36 AD which occurred in Jerusalem. He was a Hellenistic Jew and was one of the first ordained deacon in the early church. He was highly recognized for his ministerial gift as an evangelist. He was stoned to death due to his faith in Christ and was buried by a Christian but the place of his tomb was not known.

St. Lawrence: In 258 AD the Roman Emperor, Valerian persecuted St. Lawrence. St. Lawrence was one of the seven deacons who should assist the poor under Pope Sixtus II and Emperor Valerian persecuted pope Sixtus. The Roman Soldiers arrested pope Sixtus and beheaded him including his deacons. Emperor Valerian judged St. Lawrence and killed him by grilling on gridiron. St. Lawrence was buried at Cemetery in Tiburtina.

St. Margaret Clitherow: She was born in Middleton, England in 1555 and her parents were Protestant. Later she joined the Catholic Church through Dr. Thomas Vavasour in York. On March 25, 1586 she was sent to the toll-booth on Ouse Bridge and was stretched out on the ground and sharp rock on her back but her body was crushed under a door overladen with heavy weights. Her bones were broken and she gave up the ghost in 15 minutes.

St. Sebastina: He came from Southern France and received his education in Milan, Italy. He joined the Roman Army in 283AD. So that he could help Christians who were persecuted by the Romans. Emperor Diocletian appointed him as the captain of the Praetorian Guard not knowing he was a Christian. Emperor Diocletian blamed St. Sebastina for betrayal and persecuted him because he convinced Marcus and Marcellian's parents to become Christians. He converted other important persons including the local prefect. Because of this, he was bound to a stake in a field, shot with arrows and was left to die.

St. Dymphna: She was born in Ireland around seventh century. Her father was a pagan and her mother was devout Christian. She committed herself to Christ at the age of fourteen years. When her mother died, her father became mentally unstable. Her father's wicked advisor told her father to marry his own daughter. Dymphna did not allow herself to her father to marry her. Because of this, her father beheaded her when she was fifteen years old.

St. Andrew: He was one of the followers of the first disciples of Christ. He was the brother of Peter and was older than him. He was born in Bethsaida on the Sea of Galilee between 5AD and 10AD. He visited the shores of the Black Sea to proclaim the gospel. Governor Aegeas told him to deny his faith in Christ and stopped preaching. At that time, he was living in Greece but he did not follow his advice. The Governor sentenced him to death by crucifixion in the city of Patras. He should be crucified on a cross but demanded an X-shaped cross because he did not deserve to die like the way Jesus Christ died.

St. Bartholomew: He was born in Cana in the first century. He was one of the twelve apostles of Christ. He and St. Jude Thaddeus went to Armenia to preach the gospel of Christ. He converted the king of Arnenia, Polymers to Christianity. When the king's brother heard this news, he instructed that Bartholomew must be sentenced to death. He was flayed and skinned live.

Joan of Arc: She was born on 6th January, 1412. Her parents were pious of the French peasant class in the village of Domremy situated at province of Lorraine. At tender age she led French Army to victory admitting that she operated under God's direction. She was sentenced to death because she failed to submit to church authority. When she heard it, she revoked and judged to everlasting imprisonment. She was instructed to wear female clothes Few days later she wore male attire again. She was burned at the stake on May 30th at the age of 19 years.

John Wycliff: He might not be a saint but contributed a lot to the spread of Christianity. He was called "The Morning Star of Reformation" and was a 14-century theologian. Apart from Bible preaching, he was the first person to translate the Bible into English Language. He is the "Father of English prose but one pope blamed him for being heretic because he was against the papal authority. Catholic Church pope challenged him who based in England. Two popes summoned him to Rome but he was not imprisoned. He was not sacked from the church though he questioned the doctrines of the church and the life of the ministers of God. He was ill with fatal stroke during one of his masses. He died peacefully, 44 years later the church exhumed his body, burned his bones together with his books and scattered his ashes in a nearby river.

Willam Tyndale: He is the "Father of the English Bible" and translated 90 percent of the King James Version of the Bible. More than 100years he was awarded the first English translator of the Bible. He determined to make the Bible common to people in their Languages. At that time the church did not allow anyone to translate the Bible into English Language. He was accused of heresy and was sentenced into prison for one and half years. He was judged and was sentenced to death on October 6, 1536 by strangling and his body was burned.

CHAPTER FOUR

APOSTLE PETER

St. Peter died in Italy and was a follower of Jesus Christ and regarded by the early church as the leader of the twelve apostles of Christ. Peter is respected as the first pope of the Roman Catholic Church. The information about his life is found in the New Testament Bible especially the gospel, Acts, the two epistles of Paul and the two epistles bearing his name. The Jews knew him as Simeon, the Greek form of Simon. The word "Simon" appears two times and the Greek word "Simon" is mentioned 49times in the New Testament Bible. The gospel of John says Peter was known as Simon, son of John (John 21: 15). The gospel of John uses the word "Simon" 17times and the book of Acts utilizes the Greek translation "Petros" for about 150times. Matthew 8: 14; 1Corinthians 9: 5 proof indirectly that Peter was the son of John. Apostle Peter was married but his family came from Bethsaida in Galilee (John 1: 44). During Jesus' earthly ministry, he stayed at Capernaum, the northwest end of the Sea of Galilee. Peter and his brother, St. Abdrew were working with St. James and St. John as fishermen. St. James and St. John were the sons of Zebedee (Luke 5: 10). According to the New Testament Bible Peter was not educated because he was not trained in the Mosaic Law (Acts 4: 13) and it was strange that he understood Greek.

THE PETERINE CROSS

This is an inverted Latin Cross traditionally utilize as a Christian symbol associated with the martyr death of apostle Peter. According to Christian tradition Peter was crucified in Rome. The early church were harmonious in claiming that Peter died in Rome by crucifixion during the persecution of Emperor Nero in A.D64. The earliest evidence of his execution was discovered in Clement of Rome's epistle to the Corinthians in the year 90. Clement does not specify where or how he died. The gospel of John talks about Peter's execution. Eusebius pointed out that all the apostles of Christ die as a martyr except apostle John. When Peter was sentenced to death, he requested that his cross should be turned upside down because he perceived that he was not worthy to be crucified like Christ.

WHAT IS PRAYER

Prayer is the communication between God and man. Prayer may be collective or personal act using various forms and methods. Prayer is important and universal aspect of religion. Religious Historians, theologians and believers recognize the main position that prayer occupies in religion. Christian Mystic of India says prayer is vital like breathing. An American Philosopher, William James says without prayer there will be no question on religion.   The Islamic Ouran is considered as a book of prayer and the book of Psalms of the Bible is regarded as meditation on Biblical history turned into prayer. The basic definition of prayer is speaking to God but prayer is not meditation. Prayer is the means for a believer in Christ to express his emotions and desires to God and to fellowship with Him. Prayer can be audible, silent, private, pubic, formal or informal. As human, we should pray in faith through in the name of the Lord Jesus Christ (James 1: 6; John 16: 23) and in the power of the Holy Spirit (Romans 8: 26). The Biblical meaning of prayer is seeking the favor of God (Exodus 32: 11); expressing the desires of one's soul to Him (1Samuel 1: 15).

BIBLICAL TEXTS ABOUT PRAYER

- Matthew 6: 5-8; 1Chronicle 16: 11
- Hebrews 4: 16; James 5: 16
- 1 Thessalonians 5: 16-18; Matthew 5: 44
- Philippians 4: 6-7; Proverbs 15: 8
- 1 John 5: 14-15; Psalms 17: 6
- Mark 11: 24; Psalms 141: 2; Romans 12: 12
- Ephesians 6: 17-18; Luke 18: 1; Romans 8: 26
- 1 Timothy 2: 1; Jeremiah 29: 12; John 17: 9
- James 5: 16; Colossians 4: 2; John 2: 7
- Psalms 4: 1; 1Timothy 2: 8; Daniel 9: 17
- Psalms 32: 6; Acts 2: 21; Proverbs 15: 29
- Psalms 39: 12; Job 22: 27

SIGNIFICANCE OF PRAYER

- Prayer assists man to get closer to God (James 4: 8).

- It enables us to establish relationship with Him.

- It helps us to endure difficulties in life.

- It assists us to develop our relationship with Him.

- It enables us to develop the habit of compassion.

- It reveals to us the heart of God (John 17: 21).

- It helps us to be united with God and experience the relationship Jesus had with Him.

- It portrays the wisdom of God (James 1: 5).

- It brings us into the presence of God

WHAT IS HOMOSEXUALITY

Homosexuality is the attraction between two parties who have the same sex. The word "Homosexuality" is derived from Greek word called "homo" meaning "the same". The terms used for homosexual people are "gay", "lesbian", "LGBTQ", or "queer". Gay people develop feelings for people of the same sex right from their teenage stage. Gay implies a man attracted to another man and lesbian means a woman being attracted to another woman.

WHAT DOES THE BIBLE SAY ABOUT HOMOSEXUALITY

God does not support homosexuality so those who practice homosexuality are declared as sinners (Genesis 19; Jude 1: 7; Leviticus 18; 20; 18: 22; 20: 13; Romans 1: 18-32; 1Corinthians 6: 9-10; 1Timothy 1: 8-10).

WHAT IS MASTURBATION

Masturbation is self-stimulation of one's own genitals for sexual arousal or sexual pleasure to the point of orgasm. Stimulation is done through using hands, everyday objects or sex toys or the mouth. It can be practiced with sex partner. Both parties practice it together or one partner practice it while other partner watching him

CAN A CHRISTIAN PRACTICE MASTURBATION?

The Scripture does not allow adultery, fornication, homosexuality, incest, bestiality and lust but does not mention masturbation or self-stimulation. Masturbation practice by married couples is not classified as sin. If unmarried person practice masturbation, he or she has committed sin.

THE MINISTRY OF APOSTLE PAUL

Paul became converted on his way to Damascus, entered Damascus and lived there for some time (Acts 9: 19). He went to Arabia and came back to Damascus (Galatians 1: 17). From the time he became converted until he left Damascus was 3years (Galatians 1: 18). After this period, he went to Jerusalem and lived there for 15days (Acts 9: 26-29; Galatians 1: 18). When he spent 15days in Jerusalem, the apostles told him to leave to avoid being arrested. He sailed from Casarea to the region of Syira and Cilicia (Acts 9: 30; Galatians 1: 21). After 8-14days, he journeyed to Antioch with Barnabas and lived there for one and half years (Acts 11: 25; Galatians 1: 21; 2: 1). He lived in Antioch for short time (Acts 11: 27-30; Galatians 2: 1). He visited Jerusalem for the 2nd time and came back to Antioch. After his 2nd visit to Jerusalem, he started his 1st missionary journey. Paul, Mark and Barnabas journeyed from Antioch to Selecia and they came to Cyprus. They went to Pamphylia, the north of Cyprus. From there they travelled to Galatia and Derbe but Mark came home. They sailed from Perga and came to Antioch of Syira. This journey took a period of six to nine months. After the conflict in Galatians 2, Paul journeyed. from Antioch to Jerusalem and came back to Antioch. During that time, they had started the 2nd missionary journey (Acts 15-17). Paul and Barnabas separated. Paul moved with Silas and Mark joined Barnabas. Paul and Silas travelled from Antioch to Syira and they went to Cilicia. They went to Derbe, Lystra; passed Phrygia and Galatia. When they reached Troas, Paul had a vision which directed him to Macedonia. At Troas Luke joined Paul and Silas. They travelled to Philipgamothrace, Neopolis, Amphipolisa, Thessalonica and Berea. Paul visited Athens and Corinth but lived Corinth for one and half years. After Macedonia and Greek ministry, he journeyed to Ephesus, Caesarea and Antioch.

THE DEATH OF APOSTLE PAUL

During apostle Paul's second imprisonment in Rome, the epistle of second Timothy was written around AD64-67. Christian traditions about his death are few but the common view concerning his death accepted is Eusebius' writings. According to Eusebius he was beheaded by the then Roman Emperor, Nero. He died as a martyr when Rome had been burned. Emperor Nero attributed the cause of this problem to Christians. Apostle Paul was beheaded because he was a Roman citizen and Ronan citizens were not allowed to be crucified (Acts 22: 28). The Scripture does not state how he dies

WHAT IS INCEST

The word "incest" is a broad term which covers particular types of incest such as "adult-on-adult abuse", "adult-on-child abuse"; "child -on-child abuse". Dictionaries define incest as sexual activity or marriage between family members who are not allowed to marry because of close kinship.

BIBLICAL TEXTS ABOUT INCEST

1Corinthians 5: 1; Genesis 20: 12; Leviticus 18: 6; 18; 6-18; Deuteronomy 27: 20-22; Genesis 35: 22; Deuteronomy 27: 23; Leviticus 18: 8; Exodus 6: 20; Genesis 49: 4; Leviticus 20: 17; Deuteronomy 22: 30; 20: 11; 18: 7-10; Genesis 19: 1-38; Amos 2: 7; Mark 6: 17; 2Samuel 16: 21; Genesis 19: 30-36

DEFINITION OF ABORTION

An abortion is a mechanism of ending a pregnancy. Sometimes an abortion is also called termination of pregnancy. The pregnancy ends through taking medicine or surgical method. Six out of purposed pregnancies end in an induced abortion. About 45 percent of abortion are not safe and 97 percent occur in developing countries. About 73 million disposed abortion happen worldwide every year. 61 percent of unpurpose pregnancies   and 29 percent of pregnancies end in disposed abortion.

DOES THE BIBLE SUPPORT ABORTION?

The Bible does not address the issue of abortion. Biblical doctrines spell out divine views on abortion. God says He knows us before He develops us in our mothers' womb (Jeremiah 1: 5). He plays an active role in the recreation and formation of man in our mothers' womb (Psalms 138: 13-16). The penalty for the death of a baby in the womb is the same penalty giving to an individual who has committed murder. The truth is God regards a baby in the womb as grown-up person. An abortion is an issue of the life or death of a person created in the image of God. To sum up an abortion is the same as murder.

WHAT IS PROSTITUTION

Prostitution is the business of sexual activity in exchange for money. Prostitution is also called sexual service or commercial sex. An individual involves in this field is known as prostitute. Terms like "hooker", "whore" are referring to a person who is a prostitute.

WHAT DOES THE BIBLE SAY ABOUT PROSTITUTION

According to the Scripture prostitution is an immoral act (Proverbs 23: 27-28). God does not allow His children to make friendship with prostitutes (Proverbs 5: 3-5). Prostitution demolishes the soul and the spirit which create physical and spiritual death. He wants us to keep ourselves pure and utilize our bodies for His glory (Romans 6: 13; 1Corinthians 6: 13).

IS IT GOOD FOR A CHRISTIAN TO PLAY LOTTERY?

The word "gambling" means "to risk something of value on an outcone that depend on chance". Since outcome of lottery depend on chance and playing it involves risk. Therefore playing lottery is gambling. The Scripture does not contain examples of lottery but has instances of gambling (Judges 14: 12; Mark 15: 24). The primary purpose of playing lottery is to win money and the Bible instructs us about what our attitudes towards money should be. Playing lottery to get rich quickly is vain and indicates the temporary riches of the world (Proverbs 23: 5). The truth is God wants us to get money through hard work. A person who does not like to work hard will not eat (2Thessalonians 3: 10). We must be wealthy through diligence and not laziness (Proverbs 10: 4). Gambling such playing lottery covet money and the things money can buy (Exodus 20: 17; 1Timothy 6: 10)

FAITH

Ephesians 2: 8-10; Hebrews 11: 1-3; Hebrews 10: 22-23; Psalms 119: 30; Mark 11: 22 _23; Philippians 4: 13; Mark 10: 27; 2Timothy 2: 7-8; 1Corinthians 16: 13; 1Corinthians 13: 13; 1Corinthians 5: 7; James 2: 14-17; James 1: 2-4;

1Thessalonians 1: 3; James 2: 26; James 2: 18; Micah 6: 8; 1John 3: 17-18; Galatians 5: 5-6; Hebrews 10: 39; Matthew 21: 22; Luke 1: 37; 2Corinthians 5: 7; Hebrews 11: 1, 6; Ephesians 2: 8-9; Proverbs 3: 5-6; Matthew 21: 22; Romans 10: 17; James 2: 19; Ephesians 2: 8-9; Luke 1: 39

REPENTANCE

1John 1: 9; Acts 2: 38; Luke 13: 3; 2Chronicles 7: 14; Psalms 38: 18; Psalms 51: 13; Proverbs 28: 13; Isaiah 55: 6-7; Jeremiah 26: 3; Ezekiel 18: 21-23; Joel 2: 13; Jonah 3: 10; Zechariah 1: 3; Matthew 3: 8, 11; Mark 1: 4; Luke 3: 3; Acts 13: 24; Acts 19: 4; Matthew 9: 13; Mark 1: 15

SALVATION

Acts 4: 12; John 14: 6; Matthew 7: 21 Ephesians 2: 8-9; John 3: 16-18; Matthew 19: 25-26; Acts 16: 30-33; Romans 8: 38-39; Romans 10: 9-10; Philippians 3: 4-11; Isaiah 57: 12; Hebrews 7: 25; Revelation 22: 17; Ephesians 2: 8-9; Ezekiel 36: 20; Colossians 1: 13-14; 2Peter 3: 9; Isaiah 33: 22; Psalms 34: 22; Psalms 103: 12; Isaiah 44: 22; Isaiah 53: 5; Mark 10: 45; Luke 19: 10; John10: 9-10; Romans 5: 7-8; Romans 5: 10

FORGIVENES

Romans 12: 17; Proverbs 15: 1; Matthew 5: 7; Hebrews 8: 12; John 13: 34; 2Chronicles 7: 14; Luke 17: 3; Acts 19: 43; Matthew 5: 23-24; Isaiah 55: 7; 1John 2: 2; 1Peter 4: 8; Mark 11: 25; Matthew 6: 14; Psalms 32: 1; Proverbs 17: 9; Galatians 6: 1; Daniel 9: 9; Isaiah 1: 18; Hebrews 10: 17; James 5: 16; Luke 6: 27; Matthew 18: 15; Ephesians 1: 7-8; Luke 6: 37

CHAPTER FIVE

BIBLE VERSES

HOLINESS

Exodus 15: 11; 1Samuel 2: 2; Isaiah 6: 3; Isaiah 57: 15; Ezekiel 38: 28; Revelation 15: 4; Leviticus 11: 45; Leviticus 19: 2; Leviticus 20: 26; Matthew 5: 48; Romans 12: 1; 2Corinthians 7: 1; Ephesians 1: 4; 1Thessalonians 4: 7; Hebrews 12: 14; 1Peter 1: 15-16; Romans 6: 22; Ezekiel 36: 23; 2Corinthians 5: 21; Colossians 1: 22; 2Thessalonians 2: 13; 2Timothy 1: 9; Hebrews 12: 10; 1Peter 2: 24; Amos 5: 14; Romans 6: 19; Ephesians 5: 3

THE LORD'S SUPPER

Acts 2: 42; 2Corinthians 10: 16; 1Corinthians 11: 24; Acts 20: 7; Luke 22: 19; 1Corinthians 11: 26; 1Corinthians 10: 21; 1Corinthians 11: 20; Matthew 28: 26-28; Mark 14: 22-24; Luke 22: 21; Matthew 26: 26; Mark 14: 22; Luke 24: 30; John 6: 11; 1Corinthians 11: 25; Matthew 25: 27-28; Mark 14: 23-24; Luke 22: 20.

PATIENCE

Romans 12: 12; Galatians 6: 9; Romans 8: 25; Ephesians 4: 2; Psalms 37: 7-9; Psalms 86: 1; Romans 8: 23-25; Romans 2: 4; James 1: 19-20; Galatians 5: 22-23; James 1: 2-4; Colossians 3: 12-13; James 5: 7-8; 2 Peter 3: 8-9; 2Peter 3: 11-15

CHURCH

Matthew 18: 20; Hebrews 10: 24-25; Colossians 3: 16; Ephesians 4: 11-13; Acts 2: 42; Romans 10: 17; Matthew 16: 18; Acts 9: 31; Matthew 6: 33; James 1: 22; 1 Corinthians 12: 27; Romans 12: 4-5; 1Corinthians 12'12; Ephesians 4: 4; Colossians 1: 24.

WATER BAPTISM

1Peter 3: 21; Acts 2: 38; Acts 22: 16; Mark 16: 16; John 3: 5; Acts 2: 41; Galatians 3: 27; Matthew 28: 19; Romans 6: 4; Romans 6: 3; Colossians 2: 12; Matthew 28: 19-20; Acts 10: 46; Matthew 3: 16; Acts 10: 48; Mark 1: 4

SIN

Galatians 5: 19-21; James 1: 14-15; Galatians 3: 6; Romans 6: 12-14; Colossians 3: 5-6; Romans 3: 9-12; 1John 3: 4-6; Romans 5: 12-15; 2Corinthians 5: 21; 1John 1: 7-9

SONS OF GOD

Genesis 6: 2-7; Exodus 4: 22-23; 2Samuel 7: 14; 1Chronicles 17: 13; 1Chrinicles 22: 10; 1Chronicles 28: 6; Job 1: 6; Job 2: 7; Hosea 1: 10; Matthew 5: 9; Luke 20: 34-36; John 1: 12-13; John 11: 52; Romans 8: 12-25; Romans 9: 6-8; 2Chronicles 6: 14-18; Galatians 3: 24-29

VILIGLANCE

1Corinthians 10: 12; Deuteronomy 4: 9; 1Peter 5: 8-10; Proverbs 4: 23; 1Corinthians 16: 13; Revelation 3: 2; Matthew 26: 41; Colossians 4: 2; Acts 20: 31; 1Peter 5: 8

CHILDREN OF THE DEVIL

Acts 13: 10; Matthew 15: 38; John 8: 44; John 6: 70; 1John 3: 10

TRINITY

1Corinthians 8: 6; 2Corinthians 3: 17; 2Corinthians 13: 14; Colossians 2: 9; Isaiah 9: 6; Isaiah 44: 6; John 1: 14; 10: 30; Luke 1: 35; Matthew 1: 23; 28: 19; Matthew 3: 16-17; John 14: 16-17; Romans 14: 17-18; Luke 3: 21-22; Genesis 1: 1-2; 1John 5: 7-8; 1Peter 1: 1-2; 2Corinthians 1: 21-22; 1Corinthians 12: 4-6; Ephesians 4: 4-6; Colossians 1: 15-17

EVANGELISM

Matthew 9: 37-38; Mark 16: 15; Luke 24: 45-47; Romans 1: 16; Romans 10: 14-15; 2Corinthians 5: 20; 2Timothy 4: 5; 1Peter 3: 15-16

HOLY SPIRIT BAPTISM

1Corinthians 6: 19; Acts 1: 8; 2: 38; Isaiah 11: 2; John 14: 26; Judges 3: 10-14; Romans 7: 26; Matthew 12: 31-33; Galatians 5: 22-23; Luke 24: 45-49; John 14:

15-17; 2Corinthians 15: 16-18; John 3: 6-8; 1Corinthians 12: 18-20; Psalms 52: 1-3; Micah 3: 8-10; Acts 2: 1-5; Luke 24: 45-47; 1John 2: 19-27

EXISTENCE OF GOD

Hebrews 11: 6; Exodus 3: 14; Daniel 2: 28; Revelation 1: 4, 8, 11: 17, 16: 9-10; Romans 2: 14-15; Genesis 1: 31; Job 2: 7-9; Psalms 139: 14; Proverbs 1: 7

JESUS CHRIST

John 6: 35, 14: 6-11, 8: 56-59; Philippians 2: 5-7; Colossians 1: 15-20; John 1: 1-3; Luke 22: 66-71; John 5: 14-18; John 10: 25-33; Colossians 2: 9-19

SATAN

John 3: 8; 1Corinthians 7: 5; Acts 5: 3; John 10: 10; James 4: 7; Matthew 16: 23; Romans 16: 20; Zechariah 3: 1-2; 1Peter 5: 8-9; Revelation 20: 1-6; Luke 22: 1-6; Job 1: 6-12

GUARDIAN ANGELS

Exodus 23: 20; Psalms 91: 11-12; Daniel 6: 22; Matthew 18: 10, 26: 53; Hebrews 1: 14; 1Corinthians 4: 9; Acts 38: 26; 12: 16; Daniel 8: 21; 10: 13; 12: 1; Psalms 34: 7; 91: 11

HEAVEN

Isaiah 25: 8-12; Matthew 5: 17-20; 7: 13-15; 19: 17-19; Luke 13: 29-33; John 14: 2-4; Colossians 3: 1-7; Revelation 7: 13-17; 21: 4-8; Revelation 22: 3-7; 22: 5-9; Ezekiel 28: 24-26; Matthew 22: 29-33

SECTION A

OBJECTIVES QUESTIONS AND ANSWERS

1. The names of the following people were among Jesus' disciples.

A. Mary Magdalene B. Zaccheus C. Lazarus D. Judas Iscariot

2. These Bible verses speak about guardian angel except

A. John 3: 8 B. Exodus 23: 20 C. Psalm 91: 11-12 D. Daniel 6: 22

3. How many types of incest do we have

A. 1   B. 4   C 3   D. 6

4. Church history is accepted an academic discipline in the field of academia

A. True   B. False

5. The original apostles of Jesus were

A. 13 apostles   B. 11apostles   C. 12 apostles   D. 14 apostles

6. What was Jesus' purpose of choosing the apostles

A. To serve mankind   B. To give arms   C. To obey Him D. To destroy the work
of Satan

7. Jesus called Peter as

A. Blessed   B. Rock.   C. Revelator   D. Great person

8. Among the original apostles of Jesus who wrote the books of the Bible

A. Paul   B. Luke   C. Matthew   D. Martha

9. Where did the early church begin

A. Jerusalem   B. Bethlehem C. Syira   D. Damascus

10. The early church was developed upon which tradition

A. Ghanaian tradition   B. Pagan tradition   C. Jewish tradition   D. Roman tradition

11. The gospel of Christ was written for

A. Jews only   B. Syrians   C Africans.   D. Humanity

12. During the 1st century, the disciples of Christ met in separate churches

A. True   B. False

13. When did the early church started

A. Pentecost Day   B. Sabbath Day.   C. Crucifixion Day   D. Tuesday

14. The word "church" in Greek means

A. Holy people   B. Call out from darkness for God   C. Committed People   D. People who have zeal for God's work

15. How many days did the disciples receive the Holy Spirit when Jesus ascended to Heaven

A. 3 days   B. 7 days   C. 11days   D. 10 days

16. How many disciples of Jesus were baptized by the Holy Spirit on the Pentecost Day

A. 200 disciples B. 70 disciples   C. 100 disciples   D. 120 disciples

17. In what year did apostle Thomas preached the gospel in Western India

A. 52AD   B. 64AD   C. 70 AD   D 84AD

18. In the 12th century the Russian church fresco accepted that Paul was

A. Child of God   B An Apostle   C. Bishop   D. Evangelist

19. Who were the church fathers in the 1st century

A. Pastors   B. Christian Theologians and authors   C. Church elders   D. Christian preachers

20. In the 1st century Christians met in........ as a place of worship

A. Tent   B. church building C uncompleted building   D. Houses

21. Who is a disciple

A. Bible teacher   B. Church elder   C. Learner   D. Deacon

22. Before Andrew had encounter with Jesus, he was working as a

A. Goldsmith   B. Farmer   C. Fisherman   D. Scientist

23. The apostolic fathers worked between the period of............

A. 3rd and 5th century   B. 1st and 2nd century   C. 4th and 11th century   D. 16th and 17th century

24. The term "apostolic father" was not common until

A. 19th century   B. 6th century   C. 1st century   D. 17th century

25. Jesus nicknamed John as

A. Son of thunder   B. Son of God   C. Bishop   D. High priest

26. Which of the Jesus' disciples was hated by the Jews because of his occupation

A. Paul   B Mark   C. Larazus   D. Matthew

27. The following are the Biblical factor which compelled people to attend church

A. To seek for money   B. To express our love to God   C. To entertain ourselves D. To dance

28. Apostle Peter died a natural death

A. False.   B. True

29. Apostle Paul died through

A. Crucifixion   B. Illness   C. Beheaded   D. Comma

30. Who was the disciple of Jeremiah

A. Amos   B. Abram   C. Baruch   D. Philip

Objectives Answers

1. D, 2. A, 3. C, 4. A, 5. C, 6. A. 7. B, 8. C, 9. A, 10. C, 11. C, 12. B, 13. A,
14. B, 15. D. 16. D. 17. A, 18. B, 19. B, 20. D, 21. C, 22. C, 23. B, 24. D, 25. A,
26. D, 27. D, 28. A, 30. C

SECTION B

Theory

Question 1: Discuss the role women played in the early church during the 1st century (20marks)

Question2: Explain the importance of the study of church history (20marks)

Question 3: As a Christian with Bible references convince an unbeliever to understand the relevance of

prayer (20marks).

Question 4: State the reason why the early Christians were martyred (10 marks)

REFERENCES

Church history, (n. d), wikipedia. en.m.wikipedia.org

Early church, (n. d), Christian history institute. www. christianhistoryinstitute.org

Lee, Z. (2015, August 4), "9 basic reasons to study church history ", gcduscipleship. www. gcduscipleship. com

Dr. Scott, Manor, (2019, December 16), "5 reasons to study church history ", knoxseminary. www. knoxseminary. edu

The role of women, (1981), christianstudylibrary. www. Christianstudylibrary.org

The 12 apostles, (n. d), churchofjesuschrist. www.churchofjesuschrist. org

The 12 disciples, (n. d), bibleinfo. www. bibleinfo. com

Nelson, R. (2019, September 4), "Who were the 12 apostles? the complete guide", overviewbible. www. overviewbible. com

The history of the early church, (n. d), request. www. request. org

The first church, (n. d), studythechurch. www. studythechurch.com

Kelly John, N. D(n. d), "Apostolic father ", britannica. www. britannica. com

Martise, E. (2021, November 9), "What were the professions of the twelve apostles? "theclassroon. www.theclassroom. com

Who is a disciple, (n. d), salvationcall. www. salvationcall. com

Anderson, B. (2010, September 26), "The responsibilities of a spiritual father", thebridgeonline. www. thebridgeonline. net

Dejesus, M. (2016, September 6), 10 blessings spiritual fathers provide", markejesus,. www. markdejesus.com

Gunderson, D. (2020, August 16), "12 reasons you might not feel like going to church ", crossway. www. crossway. org

Godparent, (n. d), wikipedia. en. m. wikipedia. org

Famous Martyrs, (2020, July 13), thepersecuted. www. thepersecuted. org

Crossway, (2020, March 11), "10 bible verses on prayer", crossway. www. crossway. org

Hall, A. J(n. d), "The importance of prayer in our daily lives and how it can benefits us in many ways",thinke. www. thinke. org

Stanley, K. O(2020, July 12), "Why is prayer important ", christianity. www. christianity. com

Webmd editorial contributors, (2023, July 2), "What is homosexuality? ", webmd. www. webmd. com

Masturbation, (n. d), wikipedia. en. m. wikipedia. org

United church of God, (2010, July 21), ucg. www. ucg. org

Mccallum, D. (n. d), "Chronological study of paul's ministry", dwellcc.www. dwellcc. org

Chandler, P. (n. d), "25 reasons people don't go to church", askportia. www.askportia. com

yes I want morebooks!

Buy your books fast and straightforward online - at one of world's fastest growing online book stores! Environmentally sound due to Print-on-Demand technologies.

Buy your books online at
www.morebooks.shop

Kaufen Sie Ihre Bücher schnell und unkompliziert online – auf einer der am schnellsten wachsenden Buchhandelsplattformen weltweit! Dank Print-On-Demand umwelt- und ressourcenschonend produziert.

Bücher schneller online kaufen
www.morebooks.shop

Printed by Books on Demand GmbH, Norderstedt / Germany